Corey Bovell

Chicken Burger N Chips

Salamander Street

PLAYS

First published in 2020 by Salamander Street Ltd.
(info@salamanderstreet.com)

PB ISBN: 9781913630447
E ISBN: 9781913630430

Printed and bound in Great Britain

10 9 8 7 6 5 4 3 2 1

Dedicated to the one person
who can say my name wrong and get away with it.
R.I.P Barbara Elaine Bovell (Grandmother)

Chicken Burger N Chips was first performed at Jack Studios, London on 10 March 2020.

The cast was as follows:

Corey	**Corey Bovell**
Director	**Kwame Asiedu**
Designer/Costume	**Sandra Falase**
Lighting	**Pablo Fernandez Baz**
Sound Designer	**Xana**
Movement	**Kara Dee Rai**
Production Manager	**Maeve O'Neill**
Stage Manager	**Frederick Zennor**
Voice Artist	**Justin Marosa & Lauren La Rocque**
Photography	**Aeveen Barghi**
Artwork	**Fabienne Ayton**
Publicity & PR	**Alison Duguid**
Dramaturg	**Neil Grutchfield**
Produced by	**Oisel Production & Rua Arts**

Chicken Burger N Chips was supported using funding by Arts Council England

With generous support from Afterhours, Battersea Arts Centre, Morley's & The Pleasance Theatre.

COREY BOVELL

Writer/Performer

Chicken Burger N Chips was longlisted for The Bruntwood Prize for Playwrighting 2019.

"Corey Bovell is a master story-teller who oozes charisma, captivating his audience throughout."

CBNC is a semi-biographical story about me at eighteen during the summer holidays of 2009 between college and uni. It is my tribute to Lewisham borough during my adolescent years. that deals with relationships, gentrification and knife crime, but it's not all doom and gloom! Ultimately, it's a story about a young person at a crossroads in his life, seeing his world transform around him.

Theatre includes: *32 Peak Street* (Camden Fringe, Tristan Bates Theatre); *Are We OK!* (Ovalhouse Theatre); *Young Gentlemen* (Ovalhouse Youth Theatre).

Writing includes: *Red Card* (Excellence, The Pleasance); *32 Peak Street* (Camden Fringe, Tristan Bates Theatre); *Theory of Three* (The Vault Festival); *Young Gentlemen* (Ovalhouse Youth Theatre).

KWAME ASIEDU

Director

"It's the dynamic performance and Kwame Asiedu's direction that brings it to life with energy and emotion."

Kwame Asiedu is a theatre-maker based in London. His work encompasses new writing, devising, community and participation work with young people and adults. He has directed, worked as an Assistant Director or Project Assistant under directors Natasha Nixon, Nancy Medina and Justin Audibert, Stuart Barter and Rachel Bagshaw. Kwame is mentored by Akpore Uzoh, and Gbolahan Obisessan.

Theatre includes: *The Marbelous Route Home* (Young Vic, Assistant Director); *Invisible Light* (Tristan Bates Theatre); *The Jumper Factory* (Young Vic, Assistant Director); *Even with a Turkey* (Cockpit Theatre); *Stains* (Evolution Festival, Lyric Hammersmith Theatre).

SANDRA FALASE

Designer/Costume

Sandra Falase is an interdisciplinary artist with solid roots within live art performance design, fine arts and installations – their formal training was completed at the University for the Creative Arts in 2014. Influenced by the intersections of stage design with digital technology and how they engage local and wider communities, they strive to centre the infiniteness of transcendental lived experiences and marginalised stories by applying a transdisciplinary, human-centred and creative approach throughout their practice. Previously at the Young Vic as a young production associate, they worked on shows such as *The Jungle* and *Fun Home* as well as leading on design for a multisensory installation centring the experiences of LGBTQ Refugees – *Something to Declare*. Shortly afterwards. as the 2018 MGCFutures design bursary award recipient in conjunction with the Gate theatre, they later worked as the assistant designer on *A Small Place*.

Theatre includes: *J'Ouvert* (Theatre503); *This is Black* (Bunker Theatre).

Short films include: *Signs* (BFI); *Teeth* (Nottingham Primary Gallery).

Television includes: *Brain in Gear* (BBC2 TV pilot).

PABLO FERNANDEZ BAZ

Lighting Designer

"This is one of the best lighting designs I've seen in fringe theatre."

Pablo Fernandez Baz studied film and photography before graduating as a lighting designer at CSSD.

Theatre includes: *Zecura Ura "Hotel Medea"* (Hayward Gallery London & International tour); Yellow Earth theatre , *The last days of Lime house* (Site Specific London); Kali theatre, *Sundowning* (Tristan Bates); *Temoin "Jukai"* (BET); *The Marked* (UK Tour); *Nofit Circus Noodles* (UK Tour); *Cruising, Clubbing, Fucking* (Unity theatre); *Beyond* (EU Tour); *Sung – Im Her "You are Ok"* (Germany); *Suffocation* (Ovalhouse); *The Grandfathers* (Soho theatre); *Cuddles* (UK tour); *Three winters* (Emrys studio); *Widows* (Emrys,); *Warheads* (Park Theatre); *Result* (Pleasance); *Imogen* (UK tour); Rich Rusk Ghetto (Emrys studio); *Valhalla* (site-specific); CircusFest2018, Casa Festival2018, Tanzsolofestiv 2018, (Dance Festival Bonn).

XANA

Sound Designer

Xana is a Offie nominated sound designer live loop musician, sound artist, theatre maker and poet who has worked on a number of critically acclaimed theatre shows and performed in cities around the world from LA to Accra to Tokyo. Xana's work focuses on archives and embodying our future narratives and memories using tech to creating interactive spaces and manifest new visions of blackness within reality and sci fi, magical realism and blending genres orchestral noise/thick bass. Xana is featured on the award winning track 'Afronaut' on the Mercury prize nominated album of the year *Driftglass* by Seed Ensemble led by Cassie Kinoshi. Xana is an Associate Artist at Ovalhouse Theatre with their debut show *Swallowing Your Idols*, co-organiser of Afrotech Fest and publishes the childrens' comic *Afronaut Squad*.

Theatre includes: *Ivan and the Dogs* (Young Vic); *Strange Fruit* (Bush Theatre); *Grey* (Ovalhouse); *Nightclubbing* (touring); *Fairview* (Young Vic); *Pink Lemonade* (Theatre Deli); *Just Another Day and Night* (Ovalhouse); *Mapping* Brent Festival, *Blood Knot* (Orange Tree Theatre); *SEX SEX MEN MEN* (Pecs Drag Kings/Yard Theatre); *Noughts and Crosses* (Pilot Theatre/Derby Theatre); *Burgerz* (Hackney Showroom); *Obama and Me* (Talawa/Camden People's Theatre); *Black Holes* (The Place); *Hive City Legacy* (Roundhouse); *Half-breed* (Soho Theatre).

Film includes: *Ancestors Came* (dir. Cecile Emeke) and the award-winning animation *How was your Day* (dir. Tal Iungman).

KARA DEE RAI

Movement Director

Kara-Dee Rai is a Movement Director and Actor based in London, working across many disciplines such as; film, TV, theatre and visual art as well as teaching workshops. Performed on the Sadler's Wells stage for Breakin' Convention, and B.Supreme UK tour for females in Hip-Hop. Within Movement Directing, Kara creates a physical language for screen and stage. This includes shaping a character through physicality, choreographing transitions and full on routines.

Theatre includes: *Stains* (Hammersmith Lyric).

Acknowledgements

Niyi Akin, Elijah Baker, Lisa Bent, Joe Cusack, Alex George, Sáde, Nicole Jacobs, TD Moyo, Jordan Mitchell, Steffi Novia, Gbolahan Obiesan, Aaron Pierre, Audrey Pitter, David Pitter, Renée Pitter, Tyrell Williams, Bruntwood Prize, Ovalhouse Theatre, Arcola Theatre and all of the staff at Jack Theatre.

George Spender and Salamander Street.

Chicken Burger N Chips was heavily inspired by Arinzé Kene's *Misty* and Michaela Cole's *Chewing Gum Dreams.* These two amazing artist where allowed to tell their stories from their own perspective about growing up in London. Their plays are the reason why *Chicken Burger N Chips* exist and I'm hoping to inspire a young creative tell their story and share amongst the public.

This edition features the full-length version of the play which was correct at the time of performance.

'Remember always that you not only have the right to be an individual, you have an obligation to be one.'

Eleanor Roosevelt

Notes on the Text

Stage directions are in *(Italics)*

Words 'that' are not in italics within the text indicate the inner thought which was prerecorded by the actor

A dash (–) indicates the conversation has a fast pace

Lines in italics indicate that the actor is role-playing other characters.

An ellipsis (…) indicates a trailing-off of thought or delayed response.

Characters during dialogue in [square brackets] can be performed by the actor

All other character dialogues are performed by the Voice Over actors 'Jodie from Scene 3, Pops & Guy 1'

An asterisk (*) indicates the character's traits

An (/) indicates a break from the dialogue

Notes from the Movement Director

'Creating a movement scape for the show as Movement Director I will help the actor prepare to embody his character and play with physicality/ gestures with the other characters that may surface in this one man show. The play also goes into a psychological place, therefore we will be exploring for example anxiety into a movement language. As the play is taken back to a specific time and place we will explore the movement language/dance/grooves that may have been trending at that time to add nostalgia to the piece.'

Corey is going in between narrating the story and showing us the action within the story.

SCENE ONE

The stage has no form of human life present, just the key stage props, which will help, tell this South East London tale. Our stage includes a counter representing 'Morley's' up stage, a few red chairs, and a bed stage right.

After a few moments of nothingness, **COREY** *enters the stage.*

Corey – Ahhhhh London, the city, bright lights, fancy restaurants, all these wonderful things God blessed us fortunate Londoners with, to have and to hold till death do us part. To some London is their partner, their homie, their lover – someone who they adore and cherish. For me London is London. I've never really got to experience its amazing ambiance or glittering lights or even feel that soft breeze sweeping gently across the cheek on a cold winters night while strolling down Oxford Street enjoying a £10 crepe. Sitting on the open top bus and traveling through central London to see all the tourist attractions, Big Ben, Buckingham Palace, Tower of London, British Museum, even the London Eye. Sea World, War Museum, London Zoo, London Dungeon, Madame Tussauds and the Tate. No, that's not my London. My London is Lewisham Clock Tower, the Catford Cat hanging proudly in the sky seen from Blockbuster's half a mile away. Constant flashing lights and police sirens damaging my eardrums, Catford pitts where all the ballers go and play, Sydenham, Turnham and Woodpecker youth clubs on Friday evenings. 50p can drinks, the unsavory conditions Ladywell swimming baths is in, but to me, that's all I know.

Lights, bright lights, flashing lights, blue, red, green, amber, red, blue, amber, green. These lights stay in your brain until they become second nature, until they become normal until these lights become YOU and YOU become these lights within your community. We manoeuvre around the city following a format invented in 1869, and to this day still has a massive impact on our daily lives. We see a red light, we stop, we see amber and we prepare to move, we see green and we GO FOR IT.

(Stage lights change colour, with the text above.)

This didn't make sense to me until my big cousin broke it down; *Yo cuz, in ur life ur gonna come across bare traffic lights and I ain't talking about the ones you buck on road cuz. Now dese traffic lights come in three different colours and ur job is to find out who floats to you in a ghostly fashion sporting dese colours. Like… Like if man was to cut holes in a bed sheet, throw the towel over me and walk towards you, yeaaah dat kinda ting cuz. Now… the first colour, people come to you in is* ***RED. RED*** *symbolise a negative direction, why you think people use it for warning signs cuz, to stop you from getting close to what's ahead. The second colour, people will come to you in is* ***AMBER.*** *Now, when you see* ***AMBER*** *cuz, approach with caution. Like what Shaggy and Scooby Doo do when trying to solve a mystery. Last but not least you have your* ***GREEN*** *party.* ***GREEN*** *people, not* ***GREEN*** *party***,** *I'm ain't tryna sound all political or philosophical now. When dose people come into your life, go with them, because they will take you places, introduce you to new tings, and out of ends girls. Dat's why my chick's from Peckham cuz.*

Corey – Despite the stench of his medical marijuana, which often smelt appealing consumed the room which we sat in at the time. The smoke clouds descended from his mouth and into the air like a fire-breathing dragon unleashing the smoke. At first, I thought, "This dude is high" then I thought, "shit am I high," then the penny dropped, he made a valid point. People around you have an indefinite role to play in your life while holding up their colours. **RED, AMBER, GREEN.** What colour was I? What colour are you?

(We see police lights flash.
Lights help to change the scene to the daytime in **COREY***'s bedroom.)*

It's the start of our six weeks' holiday and boy have I been looking forward to this. Waking up whenever I want, playing *Football Manager* all day, chilling with the man dem going radio. Just not worrying about having to be anywhere or do anything in particular. Well actually I might have to worry about that small thing called, Results Day aka D-Day, but that's not for a few weeks. I just wanna chill and have fun, this summer.

You see, everyday apart from Sundays, cahh I've gotta go church with my parents, we all link up outside Ladywell Morley's the beacon of our South London community… I ain't talking about those dead chicken shops I've heard my older cousin talk about as well, East London is home to Dixy's Chicken, North London have Chick King, West London have *(Awkward Pause)* I dunno. But down South, we have Morley's. Morley's isn't just any food shop on the road, you see, to us, Morley's is like the Red Carpet, Hollywood, only a place for the elite from ends can step in there during peak times, when we're occupying it. We usually meet around mid-day and I always leave late, as I live close by and you know black people… they never know time. Some of the man dem are usually outside while the rest chill inside, ordering food or playing on the slot machines, hoping that £1 turns into £50, and then our day is complete. There's Anton, Liam, Jon, Grey, Dwayne, Ashley, Daniel, and Shawn. I spud them all one by one. The street is usually a lot brighter, with the lights from Ladywell Swimming bars and Riley's beaming, but they've been cut since closing down. No longer an area boosted by its community magnets but impoverished. Grey flicks on a beat and everyone gets gassed, we automatically begin to form a circle around him inside the doorway of the shop. Now the circle has been around long before man knew that Tupperware is just a fancy word for a container. I first saw it in school, during lunchtimes, the olders use to do it a lot.

(Grime Instrumental by Trooh Hippi begins to play.)

It's when we all gather around and spit bars to grime instrumentals just like on the radio, Shawn always sets pace as he's the best lyricist in our group;

[Shawn] – Mad about bars since I was 16
All the girls are loving my flow and my good weed
Everytime I step on da road I just look clean
Kicks haffi be all white, inna 9 please

Mad about bars since I was 16
All the girls are loving my flow and my good weed
Everytime I step on da road I just look clean
Kicks haffi be all white, inna 9 please

I tell you my darkest fear
Standing there, hands in the air
Screaming out Boy Better Know I don't care
Cos a man haffi get licked out his Nike Airs
Cos the plain clothes are coming
See man running, duck man down
Can't catch me I'm Sonic

Den it's back to the block
Chill and Cotch
Wait for my young G fi send him shop

[Daniel] – We just wanna chill
We just wanna hang
We don't wanna smoke, nah
We don't do dat

We just wanna chill
We just wanna hang
We don't wanna smoke, nah
We don't do dat

We just wanna chill
We just wanna hang
We don't wanna smoke, nah
We don't do dat

We just wanna chill
We just wanna hang
We don't wanna smoke, nah
We don't do dat

Nah, do dat
Peng ting, rah who's dat
BB's out, draw dat
Quick tings, yea, no chat
Man dem talk, don't act
She's got breast and back
I just waived goodbye
She's getting paged tonight.

Corey – Shawn, and Daniel are sick man, Shawn always goes first and merks it and then Daniel just comes and switches up the flow. I've been working on some lyrics myself, last time the man dem try boo me. Fuck it, lemme buss a few of them now.

When I touch mic you know it's level
5 figure deal no less, cah mi nuh settle
House party flow, one man turn rebel
Don't touch my mic, you know its pebbles

You ain't heard my lyrics in time
I shut down grime, da crown is mine
If you wanna see da gyal move their waistline
You better step back and chill and catch dis vibe.

It's contagious, moves outrageous
Gyal on da back roads still holding down pages
Da dancefloor was empty, now dere's plenty
Gyal in my sight and dey all want big fendi

So he passed me the mic, stepped to the right
My bars jumped out like a kinder surprise
Giving dem enough hype, I drop the mic
My bars weren't done, but I had a fun time

I'm a mic controller, mc soldier
I just keep going on, don't stop flowing
Now it's, off the top, man don't stop
Lyric for Lyric clash me get dropped

Cos my pen game stupid, Man think I'm cupid
I got the buffy, yeah I got the blueprint
It used to be a few quid, now it's a bit more
Get too close, jab man up like a southpaw.

I think the man dem are feeling this one, I've been practicing these bars for radio. Grey tries to bus a couple lines but by that time the circle breaks and everyone just drifts back into their original position when I first arrived here… Liam heads outside as he's the main smoker in our group which he loves… but when Shawn and Dwayne wanna smoke, Liam always starts to moan. You usually hear him say

***Liam** *always talks with smoke in his mouth**

-

[**Liam**] – Man dem need to at least bill it if you wanna smoke with me, you want me to do everything… Bring it *(Smoke),* Bill it *(Smoke),* light it *(Smoke).*

Corey – I've seen his spliffs make passer by's nose flare open and their eyes light up when he sparks it, like the face you make on Christmas day when the chicken comes out. Liam is 19, 6'2, stocky and has a head the size of a Malteser. His hands are always dirty due to the nature of his work as a mechanic. He walks with a bop in his step typical Lewisham swag.

Anton, our local footballing hero full of skill, power and goals fam. Left foot, right foot, top bins, he's got it all. He's always been that guy, first to be chosen in the playground, first to be chosen at pitts as well.

He's dragged outside by his so called agent Liam who's probably chewing his ear about his performance last week.

***Liam** *takes a few pulls on his spliff before talking, making it sound like he's holding his breath.* *

[**Liam**] – Listen hear fam

***Liam** *lets out smoke, and continues to smoke and talk at the same time**.

[**Liam**] – Fam the gaffer can't keep on putting you on the right, when you're right footed. Just don't make any sense.

Corey – Jon, my G which is short for Jonathan David Henry but ain't nobody got time for that so we just call him Jon. He's our… token white friend who loves black culture and more importantly he loves black woman, especially the yardie ones. But I gotta give it to him, the boy got serious game when it comes to woman, probably my biggest competition definitely when the henny in his system. He acts like his line is popping with other chicks but we all know it's his Baby Mother calling him. Proper Yardie gyal, every minute all you can hear down the phone is; *"You're a bloodclart eddddiot, mi nuh sure, why mi did open mi legs fi yuh"* He met her on one of the nights I decided to stay home and play Pro. Good thing too, cos… she's kind of my type. Dwayne and Grey go back to their slot machines in search of winning the jackpot today. These two are like the cramp twins inseparable and annoying, but they've been like this forever. Grey is Liam's younger brother and Dwayne is his best friend who looks up to Shawn *(Beat.)* and then in the corner away out of earshot are Daniel, Ashley, and Shawn. Them lot are like the Three Musketeers all for one and one for all type shit. They're literally always with each other, even on a Sunday. They met at center after Shawn got kicked out of school, Daniel and Ashley are a couple years older than us and they took a liken to Shawn there. Shawn should have never been kicked out he was a very smart individual, academically gifted with loads of potential, but once he did, he completely lost faith in adults and the system. For months after all Shawn would do is talk about how he'd been targeted in school by Mr Clark aka Judas. We're all just boys teaching each other how to be men in this friendship group of ours, not a gang.

Boss, lemme get a chicken burger and chips please, extra mayo and cheese in the burger boss and burger sauce on the chips… Well done as well boss… I'm leaning on the counter, watching Dwayne and Grey squander their money down the slot machines, I've tried to tell them that life is like this. The house always wins regardless how many times you try to change your approach, your tactics, revisit your strategies, or step back and take your foot off the gas. They never listen. They just keep on playing and I just keep watching, waiting for my meal when Shawn calls me over.

These lot are sat around a small table in the back, here the sunlight struggles to reach them, almost leaving them in darkness, except for a pendant light flicking above, reminiscent of a scene from *Goodfellas*. I pulled up the nearest chair and join in on their conversation. Daniel and Ashley do most of the talking as per usual, football gets brought up as United just played Barcelona in the 2009 Champions League final. A Barca team with a front 3 of Henry, Eto'o, and Messi, I thought United would be all right as they had Ronaldo and Rooney. Shawn doesn't speak that much, he just sits there, smiles, nods along to anything he agrees with and responds to his phone from time to time. Shawn and I go back… I'm talking primary school days, he was there when I had my first fight, first kiss and at my yard when my Mum gave me my first ass whooping in front of company. He hasn't always been this way, reserved. The light in Shawn's eyes disappeared when he lost his mum in a car crash four years ago, and since then I've noticed the change, but this is my boy, my right-hand man, my co-d. I'll always have his back and he'll always have mine.

[**Shawn**] – Yo Squeeze, college done. Wat you doin now? /

That's Shawn's nickname for me.

Corey – I wanna do this music ting. Uni is on the table, but I don't know anybody in Northampton.

[**Shawn**] – Dat's kinda far from ends ya know playboy. Probably take man twelve hours just to get dere.

Corey – I know. I know –

[**Shawn**] – Mr. Uni –

Corey – I don't even know if I'm going yet –

[**Shawn**] – Just gonna go up dere and forget about da man dem –

Corey – Never –

[**Shawn**] – You know you can stay on ends playboy, Uni overrated. What music ting playboy?

(Behind **Shawn** *a small* ***Red*** *light begins to emerge. Not a lot of light, just a small amount, kind of like a small red dot.)*

Corey – After carefully being browned in some full fat greasy oil, my chicken burger and chips is ready and it smells sensational. Dwayne and Grey always wanna have some as per usual they've spent all their p'z on the slot machines. I give them some of my chips, cos they're my boys, but I'll karate chop their arms off if they ever attempt to take some of my chicken burger. That first bite is always the best, eyes closed; jaw crunching away at the delicious, high in salt burger with 1% salad. *(Sigh of satisfaction)* Dam this burger taste dope; it's definitely hitting the spot. I take a chip from the box covered in the most burger sauce when I notice the man dem outside looking at me. They do this thing, every time a buff girl is approaching. So the spotter who's usually Liam stands and clocks her from afar and makes eye contact with the person nearest *(Action)*, then that person nudges the person nearest and alerts the rest of the group. At which point everyone starts looking around at each other, wondering who has the courage on that day. Let's be honest, trying to chat to a girl you don't know is a nervous experience and most of the man dem talk a good game but ain't got any game especially Daniel. After a more intense eye deliberation than the House of Common, I come out on top and begin to step outside.

No lie, the spotter done well this time, because she is wearing clothes sexier than Xena Warrior Princess on her best day. She is walking towards me, her eyes keep on gazing up, looking in her pathway, as she is also using her phone at the same time. Words aren't coming to my mouth, it's like I've lost the ability to speak. They sometimes say you can refer to song lyrics in moments and boy, one definitely comes to mind as her walk slows down, and every step seems to last for eternity.

(T-Pain – I'm N Luv audio plays the following lyrics
She has the body of a Goddess. Got eyes butter pecan brown I see you girl.)

Ooooooou she's bad she has long legs like the twin towers, beautifully crafted. Her hair is tied back in a ponytail with the baby hair edges to complete the look. Her skin glistens as if she'd bathed in honey milk, blessed by the Greeks Gods of old. I take a deep breath and step out in front of her,

Corey – Perfect timing I guess /

I've got a smile, yes. Lemme continue

Corey – What's your name?

*(**Jodie** looks **Corey** up and down before responding.)*

[**Jodie**] – That was smooth. It's Jodie. /

My Dad taught me this trick a while back when you meet a new girl repeat her name a few times, so you don't forget.

Corey – Jodie. That's a nice name

[**Jodie**] – Is it, it's just a name. What's yours?

Corey – Corey. You've got the most gorgeous smile, Jodie. Has anyone ever told you?

[**Jodie**] – Aww, thanks.

Corey – Where you heading?

[**Jodie**] – Just going to the park to meet my cousin –

Corey – Cousin?

[**Jodie**] – Yea, she's chilling in Lewisham Park with some of the girls. Might as well enjoy the sun while it's out.

Corey – Ooooo…True, true… But listen. Can I take your pin Jodie, maybe message you later and see if you're still about. Maybe I could swing by with a couple of the man dem.

[**Jodie**] – Sure why not.

Corey – Jodie wasn't even out of earshot and the man dem were already hyping, she turned around after hearing Jon's loud mouth say,

[**Jon**] *Look at the back, tho!!!!!!!.*

Corey – It was calm though because she gave me a cheeky smile. GASSED.

*(**Corey** steps back into Morley's.)*

My food!!!! Yo what the fuck. Who's grubby, scabby, nail biting, crustified, dry crack palms because they're allergic to coco butter hands took all my food. I scan the room like the Terminator and see Dwayne sniggering away with a mouth full of chips and mayo around his lips. Hunger isn't even the best word to describe how I'm feeling right now, so I just order another Chicken Burger and Chips to go and allow Dwayne today, because I just got Jodie's pin. Time to update my BB profile picture. Standard.. You see, that's the first thing you do when you got a buff new contact. *(Pause.)* Pictures… Folder… Ayia Napa… Boom found one. Thank God for the beach pictures.

[**Shawn**] – Look at Mr. Uni, pulling all da buffies. You know dat's Rachel's cousin, from primary school.

Corey – Swear down. Yea let's definitely go there.

The sound of bicycles interrupts my conversation with Shawn, as he glances to the entrance of the shop to see who's approaching. The look Shawn has is one that is too familiar, a look I've seen countless times. I put my box down and follow Shawn to the door.

[**Shawn**] – What you doing round here? I told you I don't wanna see you around here again, you SNITCH. Mata of fact get off da bike. Get off da bike before I kick you off it.

Corey – Shit, what's going on here? I know this guy. He's from ends but we've never really kicked it, I just see him at pits kicking ball, or chilling at Turnham youth club before they closed them both down. But he's not my boy boy, so I've got no say on what's happening here.

Shawn labels him a snitch because he didn't follow the codes of the streets, the unwritten code which is don't talk to the police, feds, 50, pigs whatever you wanna call them, but one must always and only say the words No Comment when being interrogated. Not this guy. This guy was in the station telling the police every piece of information he had, which resulted in one of Shawn's uncle's friends serving four years in prison while he only got six months.

[**Shawn**] – Walk… Bounce bruv, why are you still here?

*(**Amber** light revels itself above **COREY**, without him noticing.)*

Corey – Nahhhh Shawn you can't do this… Allow him, he's cool…. That's what I should of said, but instead I did nothing. I just stood there and let Shawn embarrass the guy right in front of me, besides I weren't the only one who didn't do anything to stop it. Dwayne, Ashley and Daniel are licking their lips hoping that this guy and his friends say something cheeky, so they could slap him up. Liam is standing there smoking anxiously, watching the situation pan out. He ain't the first person to set it off, however, he always has the man dems back whether right or wrong and Grey backs his brother regardless of who it is. It could be me.

[**Shawn**] – Don't let me see you jump on your boy's bike I wanna see you walk.

Corey – Jon and Anton are just like me, they stand there not knowing if they should get involved or stay out of the drama.

[**Shawn**] – Actually Dwayne take his shoes.

Corey – That's Shawn in a nutshell. Cool one minute, then aggressive the next. I remember Shawn saying his uncle told him not to trouble the guy for snitching. I guess that's why he didn't take it further, but this is bad enough. This place is becoming beyond toxic. A disease built up from the inside and working its way out from under the surface. Spreading throughout the borough becoming more apparent with each passing day. What a mad borough this is.

SCENE TWO

Corey's *bedroom.*

When all I did was enjoy the holidays, time stood still and the six weeks seemed to last for eternity. Not this time around. These four weeks have moved at a world record speed in Beijing, fast approaching the finish line. D-Day… My mornings have been the same and today wasn't any different.

Writing bars and playing *Football Manager* in my bedroom before heading out is my morning ritual and I love it, the man dem usually play *COD* with this new online mode. I've seen it and played it once, but my internet connection isn't the strongest, plus it's my neighbour's, I just borrow it… so I can't tell her to upgrade her package or get a stronger connection. The day she changed her provider was when I knew my life was over. She had a password now, I tried everything I could think of Password123 *(Sigh)* nope, Password1234 (*Sigh)* nope, Tiscali1234 (*Sigh)* No luck. The only person who really has a problem is pops the Lovers' Rock Connoisseur.

(Enter **Dad**.*)*

Dad – Corey…Every morning dis dam game.

Corey – It' the holiday Dad, what else am I supposed to do?

Dad – O, so do you pay for this electricity you are using, playing this dam game?

Corey – No Dad

Dad – Exactly me and ur mudda pay for dis, and you know how we're able to do dis. It's because we both have J O Bs.

Corey – Well I'm on H O L I D E Y.

Dad – *(Pause)* Nice to know you've learned how to spell, just hope there's more A's in your A- Level results. No Pressure… But it is time you start to think about your future son. Time ain't waiting for nobody and before you know it you'll be my age, maybe having this same conversation with your own big headed, picky head pickney. Look, one of the guys at work said him wife is looking for a weekend receptionist in her veter… vetin deh place where dem treat kitten, goose and dog. Yuh understand. It's a job and it will put money in your pockets, small steps into manhood and independence. Jobs aren't that easy fi come by right now, so any ting good… If yuh gone live in my yard past eighteen, all I ask is for either of two tings; Go Uni or go work, maybe not in the Kennel, but somewhere.

Corey – I'll think about it Dad.

Dad – Kids… I'm off to work now. Make sure you close all the windows and lock the door.

Corey – Isn't this kind of late for you? You'd usually be gone by now.

Dad – Dem closed the Black Market down in Lewisham to make some hippy place for the new Lewisham, so where mi can buy my porridge from now. First this. I wonder what's next?

*(**Dad** leaves.)*

"Why would I want to work there?"

Corey – That's pops, always telling me about jobs. He means well but I've got my own plans. He's a first-generation baby, he finds the concept of creative work hard to accept. All he's done is work hard to provide, I respect that, but I wanna provide doing something that I decided to do.

Message alert!

Since grabbing Jodie's Blackberry Pin we've been talking every single day, first thing in the morning until we both fall asleep. We speak about everything. The weather, football, cars, our families, school, college, uni, holiday destinations, music. You name it, we spoke about it. Jodie was simply amazing. I could tell from our first conversation that she weren't like most girls from endz, she was different.

Nothing like Georgina… When I thought I'd be Clyde and needed a bonnie, but this bonnie was too thuggish for me, she slapped her own cousin for giving me a hug. Then there was Scarlett… Crazy, Sexy, Cool. But more emphasis on the crazy part. Lisa was cool until she told me
I don't use condoms Red Flag!
Rochelle who I lost my virginity to broke my heart when she moved to America in year 11 to become an actress. I dunno why she would do that, I'd never become an actor.

Everything about Jodie was stable, she had no fears of the world outside endz in fact the world should be scared of her. She had goals, she wants to be a music journalist and write articles and interview artist for some of the biggest magazines like – Q, NME, and The Source. She has her dream, and she knows what her journey is going to be. Hearing all this information, made me think about my future. What will I be doing after the summer is done? My parents never went off to study at uni and we've been fine all our lives, but it's not about them and their choices, it's about my decision, plus the results will be here later on today, I can decide then. Right now I've got some new crazy bars I need to finish before hitting studio later on today. FA aka Fatal Assassinations wanna clash us live on air. A couple weeks ago, Shawn was freestyling and mentioned M-Money's name and ever since then he's been waiting to clash us.
The two biggest crews in endz going at it. This is music. Usually I'm just there in the background chilling, but this time I'm tryna spit some bars. Might even shout out Jodie as well.

*(**Corey** begins to spit the beginning of his new bars to a Grime Instrumental Eskimo.)*

Disgusted.
Man really thought they could do dis ting
Not knowing full well that I does dis

Pen and Pad in my bag everyday
On da 136 with a buff ting

Avirex Jacket and evisu jeans when I
Step in da rave on some boss shit
Cos my whole team does dis

I push keys like a Locksmith, empty the whole clip

(The beat continues to play out for a little bit as the bars aren't finished yet.)

I walk down to the spot and clock Ashley's fresh Gilera Runner 125 parked outside, green panels with a twin exhaust pipe. Inside Ashley is standing near the till, with his bike helmet on placed softly at the tip of his head, retelling the story of how he did 150 on the dual carriage way back from Gravesend to Ladywell earlier today popping 1 handed wheelies. Liam is half listening while sticking his giraffe tongue out licking his rizla to make the perfect spliff. Dwayne and Grey are standing in front of the slot machine with the lights still flashing waiting for them to continue playing. Anton is sitting next to Daniel on the counter in his football training gear, while Jon is constantly checking his phone.

I spud them all one by one as I walk inside Morley's. I see Shawn sitting at his usual table by himself. He lifts his head up, at the same time I enter and ushers me towards him. He seems a bit happier today, even offered to buy me food.

[**Shawn**] – Mr. Uni, do you know why I'm smiling?

Corey – Nope, but I guess you're gonna tell me.

[**Shawn**] – I've had a good week Squeeze. I fink I might go Yates or Hotshots tonight, before clashing M-Money at radio. You wanna roll?

Corey – Maybe. I ain't doing anything tonight /
I play it cool, deep down knowing I've been practising.

[**Shawn**] – It's on me… You decided wat ur doin playboy?

Corey – When?

[**Shawn**] – If ur goin Uni

Corey – Ooo that. Nah not yet, I'm still thinking. Pops was onto me today as well.

[**Shawn**] – Ya pops is a cool guy. You know I've been living with my uncle for da past year, and he's been looking after me properly.

Corey – He's your family, isn't that why you moved in with him?

[**Shawn**] – Yea, but he's been helping me make P'z playboy. Daniel and Ashley are down, and dere's room for one more, if ur down. /

Corey – Shawn's always spoken highly of his uncle and bragged about all the money he makes. An imposing figure within Lewisham who made his name during the early days of the Lewisham vs Peckham beef. He ain't involved as much now because money is his main focus and he don't play when it comes to it. I know he owns a couple local Caribbean food spots in endz. When Shawn turned eighteen, his uncle hired a stretch limo for us to pull up to the club in, full with bottles of Alize and money to spend.

Corey – What is it?

[**Shawn**] – Come to mine, chat to my uncle yourself playboy den we go out afterwards and you can spit them bars, cah I know you've got some new ones. It's proper calm and you can make P'z.
The world wasn't designed for us to succeed playboy, you gotta clock that we're living in an uneven society… I remember one time at school Mr Clark that Judas was like *Shawn you're a very bright boy. Have you ever thought about your future, college or uni.* Imagine me going uni, school was bad enough, I don't know how you've done college. Look around you Squeeze… All da man dem are here, in one location, chilling. Laughing. Making music and money together. Don't you want dat?
Endz is da only place dat will accept you for who you really are, instead of going off ends to become Carlton Banks. Some Preppy Don. I can't let anybody change who I am.

(Pause.)

I'll respect ur decision though Squeeze. Whatever da outcome is I'll support you 100% playboy, even if dat means I gotta trek twelve hours to see you. I'll do it. Fuck it. From the cradle to the grave playboy.

Corey – At that point, I noticed the whole room stop talking and all eyes turned towards Shawn and I. Jodie was approaching. She messaged me earlier saying she'll be in Ladywell and she'll pass by to see me. She steps into the shop and my heart skips a beat. She's amazing, definitely the best girl I've ever seen. She's been around the boys for a couple of weeks now and everyone has gotten familiar with her and Rachel chilling with us.
I stand up, give her a hug and a kiss on the cheek. Being the gentlemen I am, I offer to buy her food and we wait at a table. She's telling me how her day's been and to be honest I ain't paying attention to a word she's saying. I'm just stirring into her beautiful brown eyes.

[**Jodie**] –You wanna come mine? –

Corey – Huh. Where's your parents? –

[**Jodie**] – My dad is working late all week and won't be home until twelve and my mum is staying with her sister in Cornwall. /

I thought about how to respond in my mind, to sound cool and calm about the situation.

Corey – I'd love to.

"Well that wasn't it Corey, was it?"

SCENE THREE

As we leave the shop, I spud all the man dem one by one, Dwayne and Grey are collecting £1 coins dropping in the machine –

[**Shawn**] – Bell me later Squeeze.

We walk to the bus stop and wait for the 136 towards Elephant and Castle. Jodie lives in New Cross, Ghetto the border for Lewisham Borough. Which is calm for me… as I know most of the youts who chill in that area from woodpecker youth club. Once we get on the bus, we sit down and just chill, enjoying the scenery and cars driving by. Lewisham Borough is my home, a place where I've grown up and learned about life, the world, and a place where I feel most comfortable. "Do I really wanna go that far? Do they even have buses? What's the food like up there? They got any black barbers?" With each stop coming and going, Jodie hasn't moved to press the bell and the bus is slowly approaching Peckham, a place if you're a young boy from Lewisham you don't go wandering in and I'm definitely out of my comfort zone. All I could do is hear my cousin's voice in the back of mind,

"Peckham tingz cuz, gwarn!!"

She pushes the Stop button and we get off on Queens Road. SE15. Peckham…. She said she lived in New Cross… It's way too late to turn back now, I've gotta stay committed. Every step we take once of that bus, I'm hoping isn't my last, my palms are sweating and I become super paranoid with every passing car. The walk to her house from the bus stop isn't even far but in this instance. It is. My pace increased despite me not knowing where to go, I dunno if I was making a good impression or not, so I just told Jodie I need the toilet. Quick thinking…

Everytime I go to someone's house, there's always that feeling of "What If", like "What if her house smells, or what if she don't clean her room and it looks like a bomb shell, or what if her toilet still has shit init, because nobody has flushed the chain." We arrive at her house, she opens her door and all of my questions were answered there and then. Her hallway has a sweet aromatic lavender smell after burning incense sticks. She shows me where the toilet is, but I decline swiftly. I tell her that it was a false alarm, she leads me upstairs, into her room, where she has posters and magazine cutouts stuck all around her walls. She has legends like; Sade, Erykah Badu, John Coltrane, Miles Davis, Prince, Whitney Houston and Lauryn Hill on one wall, and then Ne-Yo, Alicia Keys, Craig David, Mariah Carey, Aaliyah and Beyoncé on the other side. This is unbelievable; here I am standing in Jodie's room while the man dem are probably chilling on the block. She suggests I take a seat on the bed next to her, I move nervously towards her, she laughs. Over the phone, I usually have so much to talk about, the weather, football, cars, our families, school, college, uni, holiday destinations music, you name it. However, now I'm in her room. My mind, speechless and I think Jodie can tell as well. She stands up and walks over to a small cupboard, she pulls open the draws and reveals a small turntable and a large collection of vinyls, some seven inches and some twelve. She flicks through some options before finally stopping and pulling one out. She removes the vinyl from the packaging and gives it a soft gentle blow, before placing it under the needle.

(Music – Angie Stone "No More Rain".)

She smiles as the music begins to play, turns and walks back towards me. I knew about her love for music, but I didn't know it was this deep. Older people usually use turntables, or DJ's and she was neither.

*(***Corey*** watches* **Jodie** *begin to dance and eventually gets pulled up towards her where he shows off some questionable dance moves. There's a nice vibe in the*

room, as they listen to the music for some time by swaying from side to side and occasionally joining in with the lyrics).

She sits back to rest on her headboard. I look over to her small cupboard and see some opened letters with university names.

"Yes, a subject to talk about, I should of waited at home for my results."

Before results day, she sent an email to Northampton uni, to apply for their Journalism course through clearing. Today she received a letter to say that her clearing application has been approved and that she has been accepted onto the course. She's over the moon, full of joy and happiness, a picture perfect moment. A moment she's chosen to share with me and I couldn't be happier for her, also this means, if I do go uni, I'll know someone. Not just anyone, but Jodie. But if I stay then I lose her. My dad's voice creeps back into my head,

Dad – Go to Uni or work

Corey – Jodie directs her attention to me.

Jodie – Have you decided what you're doing Corey?

(Pause.)

Corey – I've been thinking about this Jodie, I really have been, but I'm just not sure right about now. My whole life has been in Lewisham, my family and friends are here, my barber too. Here is all I know, it's where I feel most comfortable. I can walk down the road and not feel like I'm being judged by anybody because of the way I look, talk or dress. You know they've closed the Black Market, I used to buy my CDs, African-Caribbean themed birthday cards and patty and coco bread as well.

I didn't think that all this talk of going to uni will bug me, I mean, I only applied because the whole class was doing it. Not because I had a plan like you. I've just lived my life day to day, seeing where it takes me, not planning my future career or how I'm gonna get there. Now my dad's talking about working at a veterinary on the weekends, what the fuck is that gonna do for me. I wanna work in music, be the English Puff Daddy. Have you heard Shawn spit?… He's sick ya know way better than me, his bars are hard and the guys down at OnTop FM and Groove Radio are constantly on him to come. The problem is, he don't go unless he can be bothered, or unless me and Daniel go with him. Grime don't pay. Ain't no Grime artist reaching the top 10, unless they start making pop songs like Tinchy Stryder or Dizzee Rascal.

(Pause.)

Maybe the veterinary job doesn't sound that bad.

*(**Green** light appears.)*

Jodie – Don't be silly, we've applied for the same uni. Come and study with me. You won't be by yourself, you'll have me to keep you company, we'll have each other. Yesterday I read this fantastic quote in a book and
I think I read it for a reason,

(The music begins to fade out.)

To tell you.

Man cannot discover new oceans unless he has the courage to lose sight of the shore.

Don't be afraid of change Corey, go for it.

Corey – I've never told anyone those dreams out loud before. Here I am inside Jodie's room and I'm telling her everything. She must think I'm some weirdo, but her reactions are the complete opposite. She is sitting there, smiling at me, listening tentatively. I think to myself, go for it, kiss her, but I don't. What a wasteman, instead I decide to take my Blackberry out and check my messages. Jodie grabs the phone *(Action.)* out my hand with a big smile on her face. I begin to grapple with her until her face is in front of mine. Now at this point, there isn't anywhere else to go or do so I lean in, close my eyes and hope for the best. The feeling is reciprocated, because, she kisses me back. Not only does she kiss me back, but she also wraps her arms around me, making us fall back onto her bed.

*(**Corey** goes under the bed covers, showing some movements of sex while having the lights flick, in and out of darkness).*

So that was sex…

(Pause.)

Jodie's sitting under her covers still smiling, I know, I know, I just rocked her world, but there's an extra glow on her face. We sit on her bed and continue our conversation about uni and Shawn, she has some interesting points and actually, I think I'm starting to turn my head in that direction. I guess living a life knowing you've tried, rather than a life of regrets will be better…

Shit, Shawn's left five missed calls, I forgot, I'm supposed to link him and his uncle today.

Jodie – Why does Shawn call you Squeeze? –

Corey – It's just a nickname he came up with a long time ago. –

Jodie – I know, my cousin told me, but she doesn't even know where it comes from. –

Corey – So you've been talking about me? –

Jodie – Don't get excited. So are you going to tell me? /

Jodie leans over and gives me a kiss on my neck. Damm it. That's my weak spot.

Corey – Ooook Okay!!!! Stop it now. In primary school… A very, very, very long time ago when people used to hug me to tight. I… used…
To… let… out… trapped… Wind.

Jodie – So you used to fart –

Corey – Trapped wind!… *(Beat.)* Where does your love for music come from? –

Jodie – My parents. My mum used to sing in a couple spots around London when she was younger. Even though she never made it and became a star, she always refers to that time as *The Best Days* because that's when she met my Dad. His band was playing there at the same time, he describes the moment he heard her sing, as having goosebumps.

(The phone rings and **Corey** *answers after a few rings.)*

Corey – Yo, I'll meet you at yours in forty-five.

Jodie – What are you guys doing? I hope it's nothing dodgy, because I'm not about that life Squeeze.

Corey – Ayyy… It's not. I promise. Why you think it's dodgy?

Jodie – Because I know Shawn.

Corey – I'm just going to link him at his then go radio, don't worry bout it sweetheart, I'll call you later. Stop calling me Squeeze.

SCENE FOUR

As soon as I step outside of Jodie's house I do the 'I just had sex' dance. *(Action.)* Every guy has a thing they do after they've just had sex, either for the first time or the 100th time, but there's always a thing! I walk that long treacherous walk to the bus stop to jump on the 136 back to endz.

The bus pulls up and there's only one place for me to sit. The top of the bus. I can do this now as I'm heading back to endz, but if I were further into Peckham I'd be sitting right next to the bus driver. As I jump on, I tap my oyster card with a fat smile on my face. I guess the young male driver can pick up on my vibe as he gives me a gentle head nod as if to say, *I see you young fella.* And I respond one stop driver while making my way upstairs… I'm looking out the window, thinking about all the conversations I've had today, with Dad, Shawn, and Jodie. I guess things are becoming clearer… especially because today is D-Day.

Endz is providing us with a dry, warm Friday evening. No need for a jacket… New Cross Gate *(Beat.)* Cummin up *(Beat.)* Venue *(Beat.)* Lewisham Way *(Beat.)*. That's weird. Me, Jon and Liam was in Albertines two weeks ago for Renee's birthday party and now it's boarded up, but Wetherspoons is still opened even though something is always kicking off there… (*Chuckle.*) Flats *(Beat.)* I've noticed all these buildings closing throughout the year one by one, new flats opening, and construction work happening in Lewisham. Every other road has some sort of work going on I feel like I'm not even on endz right now, everything that is Lewisham slowly slipping away becoming something foreign. This means changes are happening. Changes that will make the borough look and feel different but is this such a good thing. My parents were talking the other day about how – soon in the next three years Lewisham could look offbeat. *(Pause.)* Changed… A far cry from what they grew up in. Change is often good when you know what to expect, but ain't nothing good about these changes.

Lewisham Bus Garage *(Beat.)* Yates (Beat.) Lewisham McD's (Beat.) Riley's *(Beat.)* Ladywell Swimming Bars.

My stop.

I walk towards Shawn's yard, and my mind is racing, is this the universe giving me a sign, a change is coming regardless and the reality is whether I stay here or go, my surroundings are due to change. They're making endz dead. Usually the man dem will go Brockley youth club in Turnham on Fridays, spit some bars, play some *Pro* and catch a couple gyal looking hot in their new 110's. That ain't happened in a while, not since it closed down, hotshots is cool and so is yates, but people move funny once they drink alcohol. One time one gyal try tell me I was too young for her, she was sixteen herself… Saying she needs a man who drives, but these times her oyster card says 16+ just like mine. Budget cuts just seem to be happening in all the areas that affect us, everything being built to keep the financial economy flowing and nothing to upraise the people already there.

This recession has already raised the price in certain shops, the last thing I need is Morley's to raise their price. I need my Chicken Burger & Chips to stay at £2. If not, then we're all doomed. The roads are quiet tonight, usually, the road is busy with buses, police cars racing up and down, ambulances and mopeds during the summertime as something is always happening, but tonight the traffic lights are directing nobody.

It's late and Shawn's been waiting for time. There are two ways I can get to his yard, I can walk down and around Lewisham Park Road or I could just cut through Lewisham Park, which is quicker. The only problem is sometimes they close the gates and I have to jump them.

Minor.

I get to the entrance and the gate is open.

Perfect.

All I'm thinking is "Shawn better not waste my time", cos I could of chilled at Jodie's for longer. I wonder if she's reaching People's Day. I bet if she does Shawn will be there like,

*(***Corey** *mimicking* **Shawn***'s voice.)*

Look at Mrs Squeeze.

As I walk down the pathway that cuts a diagonal route through the park, I begin to hear the sound of bikes riding behind me. Cyclists have emerged within Lewisham with their skintight clothes and flashing lights, popping up in batches of fours and fives. As the bikes get closer, I turn my body around and recognise two out of the three boys riding. These were not cyclists.

Wha Gwarn… Comes out of my mouth and the boys continue to ride on, now I'm halfway through the park, with another five minutes to walk, so I pull my phone out, text Shawn, Just cutting through the park.

I take my MP3 player out and flick through…

(Each song plays for twenty seconds

Tempah T – Next Hype
Skepta – Too Many Man
Young Money- Every Girl
Drake – Successful

Grime Instrumental(Eskimo) begins to play again.)

lemme finish of my new bars, so I can spit them to Shawn at his yard.

I lift my head up and see the same three boys riding back. This time they stop directly in front of me, blocking my path by surrounding me. I take in their faces one by one from left to right, shit. I recognise one of the boy's faces, it was the same guy who Shawn had robbed at the beginning of the holidays. Fuck!! What does he want?

Guy 1 – Wha gwarn fam! –

Corey – Nothing –

Guy 1 – I know you, I seen you about, where's your boy Shawn. I swear he lives round here –

Corey – I dunno –

Guy 1 – You know. Don't try act dumb fam. So where you going now? –

Corey – … I've got a link

Guy 1 – Corey yea they call you Squeeze init… That's it. Your Shawn's co-d and you don't know where he lives. Cool… Call him then.

Corey – I ain't got credit.

Guy 1 – Use my phone.

Corey – I ain't calling him.

Guy 1 – Ooh… so you don't have his number as well.

Corey – I do… I just ain't calling him for you.

Guy 1 – Grab his phone.

At this moment it feels like the walls are caving in on me. Slowly, from all directions, making it impossible for me to escape. Shit. I'm two minutes from Shawn's yard and twenty minutes from my own yard. I'm in Lewisham. My birthplace, the borough I've grown up in, the borough where I know every main road, back road, and side road. Thoughts start to cross my mind, "If I bang the dude behind me, I can run straight out the park, towards the main road. Fuck it lemme just do that. Watch the guy on your left, he's getting closer."

(We hear a loud scream at the same time we see a blackout on stage.)

Corey *appears center stage, in a spotlight.*

Fuck.

(Pause.)

Fuck.

*(**Corey** is alive, in a coma floating in and out of consciousness. The lights flick on and off acting as **Corey**'s eyes during this scene as he walks towards the bed which now symbolizes the hospital bed.)*

"How did this even happen? My day started off so good as well. Now I'm here in Lewisham Hospital. Fuck… I now know exactly what I need to do when I wake up, press Northampton Uni hard. Make sure they accept me even if it's through clearing. How did I manage to get stabbed in my own endz?

Never did I think I'd be on this side of the bed, I'm a good kid in a mad borough, I can hear Shawn now",

Shawn – Don't worry squeeze I got you playboy. Fuck. They try take my boy.

Corey – Shawn's reputation for fighting has grown in recent years, I can't tell you about the amount of fights I've gotten into with him, but we always come out okay. He definitely isn't gonna let this slide.

(Lights.)

Mum looks broken, sitting in the corner, Pop's next to her holding her in his arms. The sound of them praying fills the room.

(Lights.)

All the man dem are here; Anton, Liam, Jon, Grey, Dwayne, Ashley and Daniel. Jodie and Rachel are here as well. Shawn looks mad pissed, I can only imagine what he's thinking right now but when I wake up, imma tell him to chill, because if we do something it's never gonna end.

(Lights.)

I need to fight this. Come out of this and have a fresh start. Change is often good. Man cannot discover new oceans unless he has the courage to leave the shore. Lemme leave the shore!!

Imma tell this to Shawn. He needs to hear this, put all his energy and focus into this music ting. Yea that's what imma tell him.

(Lights.)

Because I'm out of here. The stories Jodie was telling me about uni life, meeting new people from all over the country, being independent, being able to have sex with her every day of the week, is kinda exciting. I guess going by myself and leaving everyone behind was what I was scared of. Scared of starting again, being that new person, being out of my comfort zone. Missing out on making more memories with the man dem. Losing my identity. Losing Lewisham.

(Lights.)

"Stay with you?"

Corey – I'm not going anywhere.

(Lights.)

Why is Pops crying?

(Lights.)

"What's going on here?"

(Lights.)

Mum!

(Lights.)

"Dad!"

(Lights.)

Anton jumps up and charges out the room.

(Lights.)

Liam's hands are shaking itching to roll a spliff. There's a teardrop on his cheek.

(Lights.)

"Jon!"

Can't you fucking hear me?

(Lights.)

Daniel, Ashley and Shawn are all hugging each other in a small circle.

(Lights.)

No..No..No…

This is not happening, no not today. I'm not ready to

Blackout.

COREY *leaves the stage.*

SCENE FIVE

News Headline.

Journalist – "Teen stabbed in gang-related incident in Lewisham…"

(That was the headline of the local paper printed a week later.)

Corey – Gang?
What gang?
I've never been in a gang in my life. They've gone on my Facebook and used one of the worse pictures on my page. It's a picture of the man dem and me at Fright Night last year. It was cold and I had my hood on. So I guess because a young black guy and his friends are wearing hoods, means that we're a gang. When we were really just having fun because it was Liam's nineteenth birthday. Under the picture, it read

Journalist – "Here the victim is pictured left from the middle with the rest of his gang."

Such bullshit, I know Mum's going mad right now.
What makes them call us a gang? Is it because I'm young and black? Is it because there are more than three people in the picture? Is it because the media only portray young black males in a negative way?

Sure we smoke a bit of weed from time to time, hop the train barriers, stole penny sweets from Jay's when we were younger, ride our bikes in a group and chill on the estate together. But aren't we just doing what kids do during the summer holiday?

In this article, they completely failed to mention that I'd just left college with a B in Business, B in Media and a B in Sports Science, or that I was planning on studying at uni this September. Just some short fifty-word article about how gang violence is affecting the borough from its regeneration programme. But they've failed to look at some of the major influences why we have no place to go and chill, or why we lack positive role models.

This is my London. My story. My journey. I guess I'll never get to see Winter Wonderland, or do some late night Christmas shopping down Oxford Street during those cold winter nights, as the breeze sweeps gently across my face. People do come into your life, but you can't necessarily tell straight away what colour they will represent until after knowing them for some time, and I had plenty of time to notice the signs that I chose to ignore.

No more Chicken Burger and Chips. I was too late, fate intervened and wrote a different plan for me, not the plan that I envisioned because the same place, which I call home, will be the same place where I will reside for the rest of my life.

Blackout.

CPSIA information can be obtained
at www.ICGtesting.com
Printed in the USA
LVHW041957200720
661021LV00008B/350

9 781913 630447